THE MANLY COOKBOOK

BACON

By

Chew Man-Food

Part of the Manly Cookbook Series

Also by Chew Man-Food

The Manly Cookbook Series
The Manly Cookbook: Bacon
The Manly Cookbook: Beef and Bar-B-Q

Dedicated to: Full bellies everywhere

THE MANLY COOKBOOK
BACON
By
Chew Man-Food

Introduction

It's undeniable. Everything is better with bacon. We know this intuitively because we've heard this in North American households since we were children. And I can tell you it's a fact, because as I researched this cookbook, and tested or adapted some of the newer recipes, everything DID taste better when bacon was added to the equation.

From appetizers to entrées, salads to soups, pastas to desserts, bacon cooking is simply delish. No bacon cookbook would be complete without the **BLT** (bacon, lettuce and tomato sandwich), the **PB&B** (peanut butter and bacon sandwich), the **BDC** (bacon double cheeseburger), and I just had to add the **BWBWBB** (bacon wrapped bacon with bacon bits), just to satiate those late night bacon cravings.

The four benefits of this book are:

1) Bacon is in every recipe;
2) Short, simple recipes;
3) I'm a dude, so I purposely cut down on the number of words; and
4) Did I mention bacon is in every recipe?

Warning. Eating bacon every day can be bad for your health. Bacon consumption should be accompanied by a balanced diet and regular workout routine. Nuff said.

Alright then. I will stop wasting time on frivolous introductions and caveats now, so we can get to Manly cooking with Bacon.

And by the way. This is book one of the Manly Cookbook Series. You can help us the most if you add an honest review on the site where you bought the book. Look for the other books in the series, such as 'Beef and Bar-B-Q', 'Meat and Beer', 'Chicken and Poultry', and more to come, by following us on Twitter @ManlyCookbooks, liking our Facebook page at https://www.facebook.com/ManlyCookbooks.

Yours tastefully,

Chew

PS. This book was generously promoted by The Bacon Chronicle. The Bacon Chronicle is devoted to bringing you the best sizzling recipes, the latest bacon news, the meatiest festival coverage, and much more. Go pig or go home!

Connect with them at the sites below to find out more about their fun Bacon promotions:

Website: www.baconchronicle.com

Twitter: www.twitter.com/BaconChronicle

Facebook: www.facebook.com/BaconChronicle

The Basics - Bacon Recipes

Bacon Bits

Ingredient
   8 slices bacon
Directions
   Place bacon in a large, deep skillet. Cook over medium high heat until evenly brown. Drain and set aside to cool. Crumble finely and store in a cool dry place.
   Sprinkle on anything you would love to make taste better.
   Shelf life - 1 week.

Bacon at its Best

Ingredients
 12 slices bacon
 Directions
 Place bacon in a large, deep skillet. Cook over medium high heat until evenly brown. Drain and set aside to cool.
 Eat alone or with anything you would love to taste better.

Bacon Butter

Ingredients
    4 slices bacon
    1 stick softened butter
    2 tablespoons maple syrup
Directions
    Cook bacon in a skillet. Drain and chop bacon. Keep half of the drippings. Blend in butter and maple syrup with the drippings and stir in the chopped bacon.
    Serve with bread or add to any sandwiches and wraps.

Bacon Wrapped Bacon with Bacon Bits (BWBWBB)

Ingredients

    2 servings of Bacon at its Best

    1 serving of Bacon Bits

    Directions

Fold 12 of the Bacon at its Best bacon strips into 3. Wrap each folded bacon with the remaining Bacon at its best. Sprinkle with Bacon Bits.

    Eat alone. Why mess with perfection.

Appetizers

Sugary Spice Bacon

Ingredients

    1/2 cup all-purpose flour
    2/3 cup brown sugar
    1 teaspoon coarsely ground black pepper
    1 pound thick cut bacon
    2 drops Angostura Bitters
    Directions
    Preheat oven to 400 degrees F (200 degrees C).

Add flour, sugar, pepper and bitters into a re-sealable plastic bag and shake for 20 seconds to mix.

Shake bacon with flour mixture a few strips at a time to coat evenly.

Place coated bacon onto a baking sheet or broiler pan.

Bake in preheated oven for 15 minutes or until bacon has cooked to your desired taste and crispness.

Bacon Jalapeno Poppers

Ingredients
  10 jalapeno peppers
  4 ounces cream cheese, softened
  10 bacon strips, halved
  1 clove garlic, diced
  2 Cubanelle peppers, sliced
  Toothpicks
Directions
  Cut jalapeno peppers in half lengthwise; remove seeds, stems and center membrane. Add diced garlic to the softened cream cheese and mix together evenly. Stuff each half with about 2 teaspoons of cream cheese mixture. Wrap with bacon and secure with toothpick.
  Place on a broiler rack that has been coated with non-stick cooking spray. Bake at 350 degrees F for 20 to 25 minutes or until bacon is crisp. Remove toothpicks. Garnish with Cubanelle peppers and serve immediately.

Bacon Wrapped Smokies

Ingredients
  1 pound sliced bacon, cut into thirds
  1 (14 ounce) package beef cocktail mini wieners
  3/4 cup brown sugar, or to taste
  1 dash Angostura bitters
Directions
Preheat the oven to 325 degrees F (165 degrees C). Refrigerate 2/3 of the bacon until needed. It is easier to wrap the wieners with cold bacon. Wrap each cocktail wiener with a piece of bacon and secure with a toothpick. Place on a large baking sheet.

Sprinkle brown sugar generously over all. Bake for 40 minutes in the preheated oven, until the sugar is bubbly. Add dash of bitters. To serve, place the wieners in a slow cooker and keep on the low setting.

Baked Potato Skins

Ingredients
    4 large baking potatoes, baked
    3 tablespoons vegetable oil
    1 tablespoon grated Parmesan cheese
    1/2 teaspoon salt
    1/4 teaspoon garlic powder
    1/4 teaspoon paprika
    1/8 teaspoon pepper
    8 bacon strips, cooked and crumbled
    1 1/2 cups shredded Cheddar cheese
    1/2 cup sour cream
    4 green onions, sliced
Directions
    Cut potatoes in half lengthwise; scoop out pulp, leaving a 1/4-in. shell (save pulp for another use). Place potatoes skins on a greased baking sheet. Combine oil, Parmesan cheese, salt, garlic powder, paprika and pepper; brush over both sides of skins.
    Bake at 475 degrees F for 7 minutes; turn. Bake until crisp, about 7 minutes more. Sprinkle bacon and cheddar cheese inside skins.
    Bake 2 minutes longer or until the cheese is melted. Top with sour cream and onions. Serve immediately.

Best Bacon & Crabmeat Combo

Ingredients
1 pound sliced bacon, cut in half
1 (6 ounce) can crabmeat, drained and flaked
1 dash Angostura bitters
1/4 cup plum sauce
Directions
Preheat the broiler.

Spread the bacon on a large baking sheet. Place a small mound of crabmeat at one end of each half slice of bacon. Roll bacon around the crabmeat, securing with toothpicks, if necessary.

Broil the rolled bacon 10 minutes, turning it once to ensure even browning, until evenly crisp and browned. Drain on paper towels. Add the bitters to the plum sauce. Serve warm.

Chips and Bacon Guacamole Dip

Ingredients
   2 avocados, peeled and seeded
   ½ cup chopped tomato
   ½ cup cilantro
   ¼ cup chopped onion
   1 clove garlic, diced finely
   ½ cup cooked bacon, crumbled
   ½ minced jalapeno pepper
   ½ teaspoon lime juice
   Salt to taste
   Artisan nacho or tortilla chips
Directions
   Mash down avocados and mix with chopped tomato, cilantro, chopped onion, garlic, bacon, and jalapeno. Add some lime juice and salt to taste. Serve with artisan nacho or tortilla chips.

Cheesy Popcorn Delight

Ingredients
    6 cups popped popcorn, still hot
    2 tablespoons bacon drippings
    6 tablespoons bacon bits
    ½ cup grated Cheddar cheese
    ¼ cup grated Parmesan cheese
Directions
    Place hot popcorn in a large bowl. Drizzle hot popcorn with bacon drippings. Toss with bacon, Parmesan and cheddar.

Breakfast

Manly Man's Hash Browns

Ingredients
   10 cups large chunks of peeled potatoes
   20 slices bacon
   2 large onions, sliced
   2 cloves of garlic, diced
   1 1/2 teaspoons salt
   20 cherry tomatoes (optional)
Directions
   Place potatoes in a large pot. Fill the pot with cold water until
it is half an inch above the top of the potatoes. Add the salt into
the water and stir well to dissolve salt. Bring water to a boil and
cook until tender, about 15 to 20 minutes. Drain and set aside to
cool.
   Place bacon in a large, deep skillet. Cook over medium high
heat until cooked evenly. Remove bacon, drain, cool and separate
into 2 sections with 10 strips each. Crumble one section of bacon
and leave the second section as is. Leave bacon fat in skillet and
place back onto stove. Add potato chunks, onion, garlic and
crumbled bacon to skillet. Cook over medium high heat until
potatoes begin to brown and onions are translucent, about 20 to
25 minutes. Serve hot with the second section of cooked bacon.
Garnish with cherry tomatoes (optional).

Soon-To-Be Famous Omelets

Ingredients
  4 bacon strips, diced
  1/4 cup chopped onion
  6 eggs
  1 tablespoon water
  1/4 teaspoon salt
  1/8 teaspoon pepper
  1 dash hot pepper sauce
  3 teaspoons butter, divided
  1/2 cup cubed fully cooked ham, divided
  1/4 cup thinly sliced fresh mushrooms, divided
  1/4 cup chopped green pepper, divided
  1 cup shredded Cheddar cheese, divided
Directions
  In a skillet, cook bacon over medium heat until crisp. Remove with a slotted spoon to paper towels. Drain, reserving 2 teaspoons drippings. In drippings, saute onion until tender; set aside.

  In a bowl, beat the eggs, water, salt if desired, pepper and pepper sauce. Melt 1-1/2 teaspoons butter in a 10-in. nonstick skillet over medium heat; add half of the egg mixture. As the eggs set, lift edges, letting uncooked portion flow underneath.

  When eggs are set, sprinkle half of the bacon, onion, ham, mushrooms, green pepper and cheese on one side; fold over. Cover and let stand for 1-2 minutes or until cheese is melted. Repeat with remaining ingredients for second omelet.

English Muffins with Bacon Butter

Ingredients
  1/2 cup butter or margarine, softened
  1/2 teaspoon Dijon mustard
  4 bacon strips, cooked and crumbled
  4 English muffins, split
Directions
  In a bowl, combine butter and mustard; stir in bacon. Toast the English muffins; spread with bacon butter. Refrigerate any leftover butter.

Bacon and Egg Tacos

Ingredients
  6 eggs
  1/4 cup crumbled cooked bacon
  2 tablespoons butter or margarine
  3 slices diced cheddar cheese
  1/4 teaspoon salt
  1/4 teaspoon pepper
  6 (6 inch) flour tortillas, warmed
  Salsa or 1/2 cup diced tomatoes
Directions
  In a bowl, beat the egg; add bacon. melt butter in a skillet over
medium heat. Add egg mixture; cook and stir until the eggs are
completely set. Stir in the cheese, salt and pepper. Spoon 1/4 cup
down the center of each tortilla; fold sides over filling. Serve with
salsa or diced tomatoes if desired.

Breakfast Burritos

Ingredients
   12 slices bacon, diced
   12 eggs, lightly beaten
   salt and pepper to taste
   10 (8 inch) flour tortillas
   1 1/2 cups shredded Cheddar cheese
   1/2 cup thinly sliced green onions
   1 red sweet pepper, sliced
Directions
   In a skillet, cook bacon until crisp; remove to paper towels. Drain skillet, but keep 1-2 tablespoons of the drippings. Add eggs, salt and pepper to the drippings; cook and stir over medium heat until the eggs are completely cooked. Scoop up about 1/4 cup of the cooked eggs into the center of each tortilla; sprinkle with cheese, onions and bacon. Fold bottom and sides of tortilla over filling. Wrap each folded tortilla in waxed paper and aluminum foil. Freeze for up to 3 weeks.

   To use frozen burritos: Remove foil. Place waxed paper-wrapped burritos on a microwave-safe plate. Microwave at medium power for 1 1/2 to 2 minutes or until heated all the way through. Let stand for 20 seconds. When serving a larger group, garnish burritos with sliced red peppers.

Southern Brunch

Ingredients
  6 eggs
  12 strips bacon
  1/4 cup butter
  1/4 cup all-purpose flour
  2 cups milk
  2 cups shredded Cheddar cheese
  1/3 cup shredded Romano cheese
  1/2 cup sour cream
  1 teaspoon cayenne pepper
  1 teaspoon salt
  1/2 teaspoon black pepper
  6 cornbread or medium sized bread rolls (buy 'em)
  1 cup shredded Cheddar cheese
  6 green onions, chopped
Directions
Place eggs in a large saucepan and cover with cold water. Bring water to a boil and immediately remove from heat. Cover and let eggs stand in hot water for 10 to 12 minutes. Remove from hot water, cool, peel and chop. Place bacon in a large, deep skillet. Cook over medium high heat until evenly brown. Drain, crumble and set aside.

In a medium sized saucepan, melt butter over medium heat. When butter has melted, whisk in the flour. Stir until all lumps have dissolved. Slowly pour in the milk, stirring constantly, until thickened.As gravy begins to thicken, add chopped eggs and 2 cup cheese. Cook 3 to 5 minutes to melt the cheese and heat through. Stir in the sour cream, cayenne, salt and pepper; stir until heated through.

Keep warm over low heat until ready to serve (do not boil). Slice cornbread pieces and lay open on serving plates. Ladle a generous amount of egg mixture over the cornbread, top with remaining shredded cheese, crumbled bacon, and green onion.

LUNCH

The Manly Reuben

Ingredients
    4 slices rye toast
    2 tablespoon Russian dressing
    4 tablespoons Warmest Bacon Coleslaw (see recipe in this book)
    4 slices crisp bacon
    4 slices Swiss Cheese
Directions
    Spread Russian dressing on rye toast. Top with crisp bacon, warmest bacon coleslaw and Swiss cheese. Broil for 3 minutes or until melted.

Apple-Bacon Sandwiches

Ingredients
  1 long baguette
  3 tablespoons honey mustard
  8 slices cooked bacon
  4 slices Brie cheese
  1 sliced apple
  4 leaves lettuce, washed and drained
  Salt and pepper to taste
Directions
  Cut baguette along length to open. Spread with honey mustard. Fill with cooked bacon, Brie, apple and lettuce. Add salt and pepper to taste. Slice and serve at room temperature.

THE Club

Ingredients
 3 slices toast
 2 tablespoons soft blue cheese
 1 tablespoon mayonnaise
 ½ cup shredded grilled chicken
 4 slices cooked bacon
 ½ avocado, peeled, seeded and sliced
 2 leaves romaine lettuce, cut in halves
 1 hard-boiled egg, sliced
Directions
Spread toast with cheese and mayonnaise. Layer with grilled chicken, cooked bacon, avocado, tomato, romaine and hard-boiled egg to make a double-decker sandwich.

Peanut Butter and Bacon Sandwich (PBB)

Ingredients
  2 tablespoons peanut butter
  1 banana, sliced
  4 slices cooked bacon
  2 slices white bread
Directions
  Spread peanut butter onto each slice of bread. Add banana on one slice of bread, add bacon on the other slice. Sandwich together and cook for 2 minutes in a pre-heated, buttered skillet.

Bacon Double Cheeseburgers (BDC)

Ingredients

    2 pounds sliced bacon, diced
    5 pounds ground beef
    1 large onion, chopped
    1/4 cup steak sauce
    salt and pepper to taste
    1 pound Cheddar cheese slices
    Preheat a grill for high heat.

Directions

Place bacon in a large skillet over medium heat. Fry bacon, stirring occasionally. When the bacon is almost done, add the onion. Cook until the bacon is crisp, and the onion is tender. Remove onion and bacon from the pan with a slotted spoon, and transfer to a food processor. Pulse a couple of times to chop finely. Do not puree.

Pour into a large bowl, and mix with steak sauce and ground chuck using your hands. Form into 16 patties. Place patties on the grill, and cook for 5 minutes per side, or until well done. Place one slice of cheese and 2 slices cooked bacon on top of each one during the last minute.

Grilled Deli Sandwiches

Ingredients
    1 medium onion, sliced
    1 cup sliced fresh mushrooms
    1 cup julienned green pepper
    1 cup julienned sweet red pepper
    2 tablespoons vegetable oil
    12 slices sourdough bread
    1/2 pound thinly sliced deli honey ham, smoked turkey, salami
and pastrami
    8 bacon strips, cooked and crumbled
    6 slices Cheddar cheese
    6 slices Swiss cheese
Directions
    In a large skillet, sauté the onion, mushrooms and peppers in oil
until tender. Layer six slices of bread with ham, turkey, salami,
pastrami, bacon, vegetables and cheese; top with remaining bread.
Wrap each sandwich in foil. Grill, uncovered, over medium heat
for 4-5 minutes on each side or until heated all the way through.

Super Hot Dogs

Ingredients
  1 large whole dill pickle
  4 ounces Cheddar or Colby cheese
  8 all beef hot dogs
  4 teaspoons prepared mustard
  8 bacon strips
  8 hot dog buns
Directions
  Cut pickle lengthwise into eight thin slices. Cut cheese into eight 5-in. x 1/2-in. x 1/4-in. sticks. Cut hot dogs in half lengthwise; spread cut surfaces with mustard. On eight hot dog halves, layer a pickle slice and a cheese stick; top with remaining hot dog halves.

  Place one end of a bacon stop at the end of each hot dog; push a toothpick through the bacon and both hot dog pieces. Firmly wrap bacon around each hot dog and secure at the other end with a toothpick. Grill, uncovered, over medium heat for 8-10 minutes or until bacon is completely cooked, turning occasionally. Discard toothpicks. Serve in buns.

BT Pizza

Ingredients
    4 slices bacon
    1 (10 ounce) can refrigerated pizza crust dough
    1 teaspoon olive oil
    1 cups mozzarella cheese, shredded
    1 cup grated cheddar cheese
    1 tomato, chopped
    salt and pepper to taste
Directions
    Preheat the oven to 375 degrees F (190 degrees C), or according to package directions for pizza dough.
    Place bacon in a heavy skillet over medium-high heat, and fry until browned, but not crisp. Drain on paper towels.
    Stretch pizza dough out over a pizza stone, pan, or cookie sheet. Brush the dough with olive oil. Spread the shredded mozzarella over the crust, and arrange the tomatoes over the cheese. Chop bacon, and sprinkle evenly over the pizza. Add salt and pepper to taste.
    Bake pizza for 10 to 15 minutes in the preheated oven, until the crust is golden and cheese is melted in the center.

Turkey Wraps

Ingredients
   1 (8 ounce) package cream cheese with chives
   2 tablespoons Dijon mustard
   6 (8 inch) whole wheat tortillas
   1 1/2 cups finely shredded iceberg lettuce
   12 slices thinly sliced deli turkey
   3/4 cup shredded Swiss cheese
   1 large tomato, seeded and diced
   1 large avocado, sliced
   6 slices bacon, cooked and crumbled
   Directions
   Mix together the cream cheese and Dijon mustard until smooth. Spread each tortilla with about 2 tablespoons of the cream cheese mixture, spreading to within 1/4 inch of the edge of the tortillas.
   Arrange about 1/4 cup of shredded lettuce on each tortilla, and press the lettuce down into the cream cheese mixture. Place 2 turkey slices per tortilla over the lettuce, and sprinkle with 2 tablespoons of shredded Swiss cheese. Top each tortilla evenly with tomato, avocado slices, and crumbled bacon.
   Roll each tortilla up tightly, and cut in half across the middle with a slightly diagonal cut.

The Manly Meat Lover's Burger

16 slices bacon
1 white onion, diced
2 clove garlic, minced
2 tablespoon balsamic vinegar, or to taste
10 fresh mushrooms, chopped
1 pound ground beef
1 cup dry bread crumbs
2 teaspoon Italian seasoning
3 tablespoons grated Parmesan cheese
2 eggs
salt and pepper to taste
2 italian style hamburger buns, split in half
4 slices tomato
4 slices Swiss cheese
Directions
Preheat oven to 375 degrees F (190 degrees C). Place bacon in a skillet over medium heat, and cook until brown and crisp. Remove bacon from skillet and drain on paper towels. Return the skillet to the heat and increase the temperature to medium-high. Add the onion and garlic, and stir fry until the onion is soft and the garlic begins to brown. Add the balsamic vinegar, and cook while stirring for one minute. Add the chopped mushrooms, and cook for three additional minutes. Remove pan from heat and set aside.

Finely chop 8 slices of the bacon (reserving the remaining 8). In a medium bowl, combine the chopped bacon, ground beef, bread crumbs, Italian seasoning, Parmesan cheese, mushroom mixture and egg. Mix well using hands. Season with salt and pepper, and form into four patties.

Open the two halves of the 2 hamburger bun on an ungreased cookie sheet. Place one beef patty on each half, and cover each with one slice of tomato, 2 slices of the reserved bacon and one slice of

Swiss cheese. Bake for 25 minutes in the preheated oven, or until meat has cooked through.

SALADS

Warmest Bacon Coleslaw

Ingredients
  6 slices thick-cut bacon
  1 tablespoon olive oil
  ½ onion, sliced
  ¼ cup cider vinegar
  ¼ cup water
  4 drops Worcestershire sauce
  2 tablespoons brown sugar
  ½ teaspoon celery seeds
  6 cups shredded cabbage
Directions
Cook thick-cut bacon in olive oil; drain and crumble. Keep drippings. Add onion, cider vinegar, water, Worcestershire sauce, brown sugar and celery seeds to the drippings. Toss with shredded cabbage and add the bacon.

BLT Chicken Salad

Ingredients
   3 cups chopped cooked chicken breast
   8 slices bacon
   3/4 cup mayonnaise
   2 stalks celery, chopped
   2 tablespoons chopped green onion
   1 cup chopped fresh tomato
   1 dash Angostura bitters
   1 tablespoon chopped fresh parsley
   1 teaspoon lemon juice
   Salt and pepper to taste
   20 leaves spring mix lettuce
   1 avocado - peeled, seeded and sliced
Directions
Place bacon in a large, deep skillet. Cook over medium high heat until evenly brown. Drain, crumble and set aside to cool.

Prepare the dressing by mixing together the mayonnaise, parsley, green onions, lemon juice, bitters, salt and pepper.

In a medium bowl, stir together the chicken breast, tomatoes and bacon. Pour dressing over chicken mixture and toss well to coat. Refrigerate until chilled; serve over spring mix leaves and garnish with avocado slices.

Green Beans au Bacon

Ingredients
  4 slices bacon, diced
  1/2 white onion, minced
  1 pound fresh cut green beans
  1/2 teaspoon cayenne pepper flakes
  1 clove garlic, diced
  1/2 cup boiling water
  1/2 tablespoon butter
  1 teaspoon lemon juice
  salt and pepper to taste
Directions
  Cook the bacon in a large, deep skillet over medium-high heat until crisp, about 10 minutes. Remove the bacon with a slotted spoon and drain on a paper towel-lined plate; return the skillet with the remaining bacon grease to the stove.

  Cook the onion in the bacon drippings until soft, 5 to 7 minutes. Stir in the green beans, garlic and cayenne flakes; cook another 2 minutes.

  Pour the boiling water into the skillet and cover the skillet immediately; steam for about 15 minutes, shaking the skillet occasionally to keep the beans from sticking to the bottom.

  Add the butter, lemon juice, salt, and pepper; cook and stir until the butter is melted, 3 to 5 minutes.

  Sprinkle the cooked bacon over the beans to serve.

Spinach Ranch Salad

Ingredients
   4 cups baby spinach, rinsed and dried
   1/2 cup cucumber
   1 cup broccoli florets
   1/3 cup feta cheese, crumbled
   1/3 cup Parmesan cheese, grated
   1/4 red onion, chopped
   1 clove garlic, diced finely
   2 small, cooked chicken breast, cut into small pieces
   4 slices of Bacon at its Best, crumbled
   bacon bits
   1/2 cup ranch dressing
Directions

Toss together spinach, cucumber, broccoli, feta, Parmesan onion, garlic, chicken, and bacon in a large bowl. Pour dressing over salad, and gently toss again. Sprinkle bacon bits and serve immediately.

Bacon Broccoli Salad

Ingredients
  10 bacon strips, cooked and crumbled
  1 cup fresh broccoli florets, cleaned and steamed slightly (under 2 minutes)
  1/2 cup raisins
  1/2 cup sunflower seeds
  1/2 cup mayonnaise
  1/4 cup sugar
  2 tablespoons vinegar
Directions
  In a medium bowl, combine bacon, broccoli, raisins and sunflower seeds; set aside. Mix together mayonnaise, sugar and vinegar; pour over broccoli mixture and toss to coat. Cover and chill for 1 hour. Stir before serving.

BLT Mac' an' Cheese Salad

Ingredients
2 1/2 cups uncooked macaroni pasta
6 cups torn romaine
1 1/2 cups cubed cooked chicken breast
1 medium tomato, diced
6 bacon strips, cooked and crumbled
1/3 cup mayonnaise
1/4 cup water
1 tablespoon barbecue sauce
1 1/2 teaspoons white vinegar
1/4 teaspoon pepper
1/2 cup grated cheddar cheese
Directions
Cook pasta according to package directions. Drain and add grated cheese.

In a large serving bowl, combine the pasta, romaine, chicken, tomato and bacon. In a small bowl, whisk together the mayonnaise, water, barbecue sauce, vinegar and pepper. Pour over pasta mixture; toss to coat evenly.

Serve immediately.

Seven Layer 'Baconized' Salad

Ingredients
  1 pound bacon
  1 large head iceberg lettuce - rinsed, dried, and chopped
  1 red onion, chopped
  1 (10 ounce) package frozen green peas, thawed
  10 ounces shredded Cheddar cheese
  1 cup chopped cauliflower
  1 1/4 cups mayonnaise
  2 tablespoons white sugar
  2/3 cup grated Parmesan cheese
Directions
Place bacon in a large, deep skillet. Cook over medium high heat until evenly brown. Crumble and set aside. In a large flat bowl, place the chopped lettuce and top with a layer of onion, peas, shredded cheese, cauliflower and bacon.

Prepare the dressing by whisking together the mayonnaise, sugar and Parmesan cheese. Drizzle over salad and refrigerate until chilled.

SOUPS and SEAFOOD

Shrimp du George

Ingredients
   16 Jumbo shrimp
   8 ounces provolone cheese, cut into 16 strips
   1/4 cup green Chile peppers, diced
   1/4 cup sweet red peppers, diced
   16 slices bacon
   1/3 cup barbecue sauce
Directions
Peel, de-vein and butterfly the shrimp. (To butterfly shrimp: Split shrimp down the center, cutting almost completely through.)

Insert a strip of provolone cheese 1 teaspoon of the diced green chilies and 1 teaspoon of diced sweet red peppers into each shrimp. Fold over the shrimp and wrap with a half strip of bacon. Secure with toothpicks.

Cook shrimp on grill, basting with your favorite barbecue sauce, until bacon is cooked and shrimp is pink.

Kiss the Shrimp (with Bacon, what else?)

Ingredients
   1 (8 ounce) package Monterey Jack cheese, cut into strips
   40 large shrimp - peeled, deveined and butterflied
   20 slices bacon, cut in half
Directions
Preheat the oven to 450 degrees F (220 degrees C).

Place a small piece of cheese into the butterflied opening of each shrimp. Wrap half of a slice of bacon around each one to conceal the cheese, securing with toothpicks.

Place on a cookie sheet. Bake for 10 to 15 minutes in the preheated oven, until bacon is browned.

Bacon and Potato Soup

Ingredients
   6 thick slices bacon
   1 1/2 teaspoons olive oil
   1/2 cup chopped onion
   1/2 cup chopped carrots
   1 stalk celery, chopped
   4 cups low fat, low sodium chicken broth
   4 cups cubed potatoes
   1/8 teaspoon cayenne pepper
   1/2 cup shredded Cheddar cheese
   1/2 teaspoon kosher salt
   2 tomatoes, diced

Directions

Cook bacon until crisp in 3-quart saucepan, remove and drain well on paper towels. Discard bacon grease and wipe pan thoroughly with paper towel.

In a separate pan, prepare vegetables. Add olive oil to saucepan and add onion, carrot, tomatoes and celery as they are cut up. Sauté until onion is soft but not brown, about 3 to 4 minutes.

Stir in chicken broth, potatoes, and pepper; bring to a boil, reduce heat, and simmer, covered, until potatoes are tender, about 10-15 minutes.

Stir in cheese, heating just until melted—do not boil. Chop bacon and add to soup. Adjust seasoning to taste by adding salt, if desired. Serve right away.

BLT Soup

Ingredients
   5 slices bacon, diced
   2 tablespoons margarine
   3 1/2 cups iceberg lettuce, julienned
   5/8 cup all-purpose flour
   3 1/2 cups hot water
   1 tablespoon chicken soup base
   3/4 cup chopped tomatoes
   1 pinch ground nutmeg
   1 pinch cayenne pepper
   1 cup hot half-and-half cream
Directions
In a heavy 3-quart saucepan cook bacon over medium heat until lightly browned, about 10 minutes. Do not drain fat. Stir in the margarine and heat until melted. Add lettuce and sauté for 2 minutes over medium heat. Whisk in the flour and heat stirring constantly until evenly cooked, about 3 minutes. Remove from heat and stir in the hot water, chicken soup base and tomato. Season with nutmeg and cayenne. Reheat the soup to boiling, stirring frequently. Reduce to a simmer and cook for about 6 minutes, stirring occasionally until thickened. Stir in the half and half and serve hot.

Venison Chili

Ingredients
4 tablespoons unsalted butter
1 red onion, chopped
4 cloves garlic, minced
4 tablespoons dark brown sugar
3 cups red wine
4 tablespoons red wine vinegar
4 tablespoons tomato paste
4 cups low-sodium chicken broth
1 teaspoon ground cumin
1/2 teaspoon cayenne pepper
1/2 teaspoon chili powder
2 tablespoons chopped fresh cilantro
salt to taste
4 tablespoons canola oil
12 slices cooked bacon, diced
2 pounds venison stew meat, trimmed and finely diced
2 cups black beans, cooked and drained
Directions
Melt the butter in a large pot over medium heat. Stir in the onion and garlic, and sauté for 3 to 4 minutes. Stir in the brown sugar and sauté for 2 to 3 more minutes. Then stir in the red wine, vinegar, tomato paste, chicken stock, cumin, cayenne pepper, chili powder, cilantro and salt. Simmer for 30 to 35 minutes, or until the mixture is reduced by about half. Heat the oil in a large skillet over medium-high heat. Stir in the bacon and fry for 3 to 4 minutes, or until the bacon is browned. Move the bacon to one side of the skillet and add the venison to the empty side of the skillet. Season the meat with salt to taste and sauté the meat for 15 minutes, or until well browned. Stir in the beans and toss all together. Transfer this mixture to the simmering pot. Mix

everything together thoroughly and let simmer for about 20 more minutes.

Chili Colorado

Ingredients
   3 tablespoons all-purpose flour
   1 1/2 pounds boneless pork, cut into 1 inch cubes
   1 tablespoon bacon drippings, or vegetable oil
   1 tablespoon vegetable oil
   1 tablespoon all-purpose flour
   1/4 cup chopped onion
   1 (4 ounce) can tomato sauce
   2 tablespoons chili powder
   1 teaspoon cumin
   1/2 teaspoon garlic powder
   salt and black pepper to taste
   3 cups water
Directions
Place 3 tablespoons flour in a plastic bag. Add pork and shake to lightly coat with flour. Set aside. Heat bacon drippings and vegetable oil in a Dutch oven over medium high heat. Add pork and cook until meat is evenly browned, about 5 to 8 minutes. Stir in 1 tablespoon flour, and cook 3 minutes.

Stir in the onion, tomato sauce, Chile powder, cumin, garlic powder, salt, pepper, and water. Bring to a boil, then reduce heat to medium low and simmer until pork is just falling apart, about 1-1/2 to 2 hours.

ENTREES

The Manly Hunter-Style Chicken

Ingredients
  4 tablespoons olive oil
  1 (3 pound) whole chicken, cut into pieces
  8 slices bacon, diced
  2 onions, chopped
  2 cloves garlic, diced
  1 cup fresh sliced mushrooms
  1 tablespoon chopped fresh parsley
  1 tablespoon chopped fresh basil
  1 teaspoon salt
  Freshly ground black pepper
  1 cup white wine
  1 pound tomatoes, diced
Directions
  Heat oil in a large skillet; brown the chicken then remove from skillet. Add bacon and sauté over medium heat for about 2 minutes. Add onions, garlic and mushrooms and continue to sauté until onions are translucent.

  Return chicken to skillet; sprinkle with parsley, basil, salt and pepper. Add wine and tomatoes. Cover and let simmer on lower heat for 25 to 30 minutes, turning chicken once during cooking. Remove chicken from skillet and pour sauce over chicken.

  Serve hot and garnish with parsley.

Party Bacon Chicken

Ingredients
    8 skinless, boneless chicken breasts
    8 slices bacon
    8 ounces cooked shredded beef
    1 1/2 cup sour cream
    2 (21.5 ounce) cans condensed cream of chicken soup
    2 avocados, peeled, seeded and sliced
Directions
    Spread beef into the bottom of 2 greased 8 inch square baking dishes.
    Wrap each chicken breast with 1 strip of bacon, and lay on top of beef.
    Mix together undiluted soup and sour cream. Pour over chicken.
    Bake at 350 degrees F (175 degrees C) for 45 minutes to 1 hour.
    Serve with avocado as garnish.

Ranch Bacon Chicken

Ingredients
  1 pound thick cut bacon
  1 onion, chopped
  1 tablespoon olive oil
  6 skinless, boneless chicken breast halves
  1/2 cup stir-fry sauce
  1 cup Ranch-style salad dressing
  1 cup grated Parmesan cheese
  1/2 cup grated Romano cheese
  Preheat oven to 350 degrees F (175 degrees C).
Directions
Heat a large skillet to medium heat and fry bacon until crisp. Drain and pat dry with paper towels; set aside. In the same skillet, sauté onion in bacon fat until tender. Add to bacon and set aside.

In a separate large skillet, heat oil over medium high heat and brown chicken breasts. Place browned chicken in a lightly greased 9x13 inch baking dish; pour stir-fry sauce over chicken, then spoon salad dressing onto each breast. Sprinkle with cheese, and top with the bacon mixture.

Bake in preheated oven for 30 minutes or until chicken is cooked through and juices run clear.

Garnish with bacon bits and Parmesan cheese. Serve hot.

Pasta Carbonara

Ingredients
  1/2 pound bacon, cut into small pieces
  4 eggs, room temperature
  1/4 cup heavy cream at room temperature
  1 cup grated Parmesan cheese
  16 ounces dry fettuccine pasta
  1/4 cup butter, softened
  1/4 cup chopped parsley
  ground black pepper to taste
Directions
Cook bacon until crisp. Drain on paper towels. In medium bowl beat together eggs and cream just until blended. Stir in cheese and set aside.

Cook pasta according to package directions. Drain and return to pan. Toss with butter until it is melted. Add bacon and cheese mixture and toss gently until mixed and well cooked.

Filet Mignon with Bacon Cream Sauce

Ingredients
   4 (4 ounce) beef tenderloin filets
   1 teaspoon olive oil
   5 slices bacon, chopped
   1 tablespoon butter
   4 shallots, diced
   1/4 cup half-and-half cream
   salt and pepper to taste
Directions
Preheat an outdoor grill for medium-high heat, and lightly oil the grate. Brush the filets with olive oil, and cook on the preheated grill to desired doneness (about 4 minutes per side for medium rare).

An instant-read thermometer inserted into the center should read 130 degrees F (54 degrees C). Set the steaks aside on a platter tented with aluminum foil to rest.

While the steaks are resting, prepare the sauce: cook and stir the chopped bacon in a small saucepan over medium heat until the bacon pieces are crisp, 3 to 5 minutes. Stir in the butter and shallots, and cook and stir until the shallots are soft and translucent, about 5 minutes more. Stir in the half-and-half, bring the mixture to a simmer over medium-low heat, and cook, stirring occasionally, until the sauce is slightly thickened, about 8 minutes. Season to taste with salt and pepper, and serve over the steaks.

Feta Cheese and Bacon Stuffed Chicken Breasts

Ingredients
   8 tablespoons olive oil
   2 teaspoons lemon juice
   4 cloves crushed garlic
   1 tablespoon dried oregano
   salt and pepper to taste
   4 skinless, boneless chicken breasts, marinated with 1 tablespoon vinegar and 2 tablespoons chicken seasoning
   4 slices feta cheese
   8 slices bacon, fried and drained
   Directions
   Preheat oven to 350 degrees F (175 degrees C).

   In a small bowl combine the oil, lemon juice, garlic, oregano, salt and pepper. Mix together. Place chicken in a 9x13 inch baking dish and pour oil mixture over chicken.

   Stuff each chicken breast with 1 slice feta cheese and 2 slices of bacon. Secure open sides with toothpicks. Bake uncovered at 350 degrees F (175 degrees C) for 30 to 35 minutes. Serve hot.

Seriously Tasty Home-Made Fried Chicken

Ingredients
  1 (4 pound) whole chicken, cut into 6 pieces
  4 cups buttermilk
  1 teaspoon salt
  1 teaspoon freshly ground black pepper
  1/4 teaspoon cayenne pepper
  1/4 teaspoon dried thyme
  2 cups all-purpose flour
  1/2 cup bacon bits
  1 teaspoon white sugar
  5 cups shortening for frying
  1/4 cup bacon grease (yeah!)

Place the cut up chicken into a large re-sealable bag or a 9x13 inch casserole dish. Pour the buttermilk over the chicken, seal or cover and refrigerate for 24 hours.

Remove the chicken from the buttermilk. In a bowl, stir together the salt, black pepper, cayenne pepper, thyme, flour and sugar; pour onto a plate.

Heat the shortening and bacon drippings in a large skillet or electric skillet to 365 degrees F (185 degrees C). Dredge the chicken in the flour mixture and place it into the hot fat. Fry on one side for 10 minutes, then turn and fry 10 minutes on the reverse side. If softer skin is desired, cover the skillet for the last 10 minutes. Remove and drain on paper towels of brown paper grocery bags. (The smaller pieces will be finished first. The chicken is done when the juices run clear.)

Place in a re-sealable bag with bacon bits and shake. Serve hot.

Rolled Flank Steak

Ingredients
  1 (2 pound) beef flank steak
  1/4 cup soy sauce
  2 table spoons stir fry sauce
  1/2 cup olive oil
  2 teaspoons steak seasoning
  8 ounces thinly sliced provolone cheese
  8 slices thick cut bacon
  1/2 cup fresh spinach leaves
  1/2 cup sliced mushrooms
  1/2 red bell pepper, seeded and cut into strips
Directions
  Place the flank steak on a cutting board with the short end closest to you. Starting from one of the long sides, cut through the meat horizontally to within 1/2 inch of the opposite edge. (You can also ask your butcher to butterfly the flank steak for you instead of cutting it yourself.)

  Mix the soy sauce, stir fry sauce, olive oil, and steak seasoning together in a gallon-sized resealable plastic bag. Marinate flank steak in the refrigerator overnight and for a minimum of 6 hours.

  Preheat oven to 350 degrees F (175 degrees C). Grease a glass baking dish. Lay out the flank steak flat in front of you with the grain of the meat running from left to right. Layer the provolone across the steak, leaving a 1-inch border. Arrange the bacon, spinach, red pepper, and mushrooms across the cheese covered steak in stripes running in the same direction as the grain of the meat. Roll the flank steak up and away from you, so that when the roll is cut into the pinwheel shape, each of the filling ingredients can be seen. Roll firmly, but be careful not to squeeze the fillings out the ends. Once rolled, tie every 2 inches with kitchen twine.

Place in prepared baking dish, and bake in preheated oven for one hour, or until the internal temperature reaches 145 degrees F (65 degrees C). Remove from the oven and let rest for 5 to 10 minutes before cutting into 1 inch slices. Remember to remove the twine before serving!

Spaghetti Carbonara

Ingredients
  1 pound spaghetti
  1 pound bacon, chopped
  4 eggs, well beaten
  1 cup grated Parmesan cheese
  1/2 cup grated Romano cheese
  1/4 cup olive oil
Directions
Bring a large pot of lightly salted water to a boil. Add pasta and cook for 8 to 10 minutes or until al dente; drain, shock with ice cold water, then drain cold water.

Meanwhile, place bacon in a large, deep skillet. Cook over medium high heat until evenly brown. Drain and keep some of the drippings, crumble bacon and set aside.

Scramble eggs in bacon drippings.

Place spaghetti in a large bowl. Pour in olive oil, and mix well; use enough to just moisten spaghetti. Stir in bacon, eggs, Romano and Parmesan cheese. Serve immediately.

Spaghetti with Salami and Bacon

Ingredients
  1 (16 ounce) package uncooked spaghetti
  2 tablespoons olive oil
  1 tablespoon butter
  1/4 pound hard salami, diced
  2 slices bacon, chopped
  1 clove garlic, chopped
  1 leek, thinly sliced
  salt and pepper, to taste
  2 tablespoons chopped fresh basil
  2 tomatoes, diced
  4 tablespoons grated Parmesan cheese
Directions
Bring a large pot of lightly salted water to a boil. Cook pasta in boiling water for 8 to 10 minutes or until al dente; drain.

Meanwhile, heat the olive oil and butter in a large skillet over medium heat. Place salami and bacon in the skillet; cook until just starting to crisp. Stir in garlic and leek; season with salt and pepper, and cook 2 minutes more. Stir in tomatoes and 1 tablespoon basil; cook 1 minute more.

Mix the cooked pasta into the contents of the skillet, along with 3 tablespoons Parmesan. Serve topped with remaining Parmesan and basil.

Tangy Sweet Spareribs

Ingredients
  1/4 cup bacon drippings
  3 pounds pork spareribs
  1 tablespoon garlic salt
  1 teaspoon black pepper
  1/4 cup prepared mustard
  1/4 cup light molasses
  1/4 cup soy sauce
  3 tablespoons vinegar
  2 tablespoons Worcestershire sauce
  2 teaspoons hot pepper sauce
  1/2 cup bacon bits
Directions
Preheat oven to 350 degrees F (175 degrees C).

Heat bacon drippings in a large, heavy skillet over medium heat. Place spareribs in the skillet, and brown on each side for about 5 minutes. Season with garlic salt and pepper.

In a medium bowl, mix mustard, molasses, soy sauce, vinegar, Worcestershire sauce, and hot pepper sauce. Place browned ribs in a large baking dish. Cover with the mustard sauce mixture.

Bake 2 ½ to 3 hours in the preheated oven, basting occasionally with the sauce mixture, to an internal temperature of 160 degrees F (70 degrees C).

Pour bacon bits over finished meat when serving.

BT Macaroni Casserole

Ingredients
    4 cups cooked elbow macaroni
    1 (14.5 ounce) can diced tomatoes, drained
    1 (10 ounce) can diced tomatoes and green chilies, not drained
    4 ounces shredded Colby- Monterey Jack cheese
    4 ounces Cheddar cheese
    12 bacon strips, cooked and crumbled
Directions
    In a greased 11-in. x 7-in. x 2-in. microwave-safe dish, combine the macaroni, tomatoes, 2/3 of the bacon and 1 1/2 cup cheese; mix well. Cover and microwave on high for 3 minutes; stir. Cover and heat for 1 minute longer. Sprinkle with remaining bacon and cheese. Microwave, uncovered, for 30-45 seconds or until cheese is melted. Let stand for 5 minutes before serving.

The Hunter's Stew

Ingredients
  6 thick slices hickory-smoked bacon
  1 pound kielbasa sausage, sliced into 1/2 inch pieces
  1 pound cubed pork stew meat
  1/4 cup all-purpose flour
  3 cloves garlic, chopped
  1 onion, diced
  2 carrots, diced
  1 1/2 cups sliced fresh mushrooms
  4 cups shredded green cabbage
  1 (16 ounce) jar sauerkraut, rinsed and well drained
  1/4 cup dry red wine
  2 bay leaves
  1 teaspoon dried basil
  1 teaspoon dried marjoram
  1 tablespoon sweet paprika
  1/4 teaspoon salt
  1/8 teaspoon ground black pepper
  1/8 teaspoon caraway seed, crushed
  1 pinch cayenne pepper
  1/2 ounce dried mushrooms
  1 dash bottled hot pepper sauce
  1 dash Worcestershire sauce
  1 dash Angostura bitters
  1 teaspoon stir fry sauce
  5 cups beef stock
  2 tablespoons canned tomato paste
  1 cup canned diced tomatoes
Directions
Preheat the oven to 350 degrees F (175 degrees C).

Heat a large pot over medium heat. Add the bacon and kielbasa; cook and stir until the bacon has rendered its fat and sausage is lightly browned. Use a slotted spoon to remove the meat and transfer to a large casserole dish.

Coat the cubes of pork lightly with flour and fry them in the bacon drippings over medium-high heat until golden brown. Use a slotted spoon to transfer the pork to the casserole. Add the garlic, onion, carrots, fresh mushrooms, cabbage and sauerkraut. Reduce heat to medium; cook and stir until the carrots are soft, about 10 minutes.

Do not let the vegetables brown.

Deglaze the pan by pouring in the red wine and stirring to loosen all of the bits of food and flour that are stuck to the bottom. Season with the bay leaf, basil, marjoram, paprika, salt, pepper, caraway seeds and cayenne pepper; cook for 1 minute.

Mix in the dried mushrooms, hot pepper sauce, Worcestershire sauce, stir fry sauce, bitters, beef stock, tomato paste and tomatoes. Heat through just until boiling. Pour the vegetables and all of the liquid into the casserole dish with the meat. Cover with a lid.

Bake in the preheated oven for 2 1/2 to 3 hours, until meat is very tender.

Serve with bread rolls and bacon butter.

Meaty Baked Beans

Ingredients
  1 pound thick cut bacon
  1 pound lean ground beef
  1/2 pound sage pork sausage
  2 cloves garlic, crushed
  1 large onion, cut into 1/2-inch pieces
  1 cup dark brown sugar
  1 cup real maple syrup
  1 cup ketchup
  1/4 cup prepared yellow mustard
  1/2 cup chipotle sauce
  2 (16 ounce) cans baked beans
  1 (16 ounce) can kidney beans
  1 (16 ounce) can black beans
  1 (16 ounce) can pinto beans
  1 (16 ounce) can lentil beans
  1 tablespoon chili powder
  salt to taste
Directions
Place bacon in a large skillet over medium-high heat and cook until evenly brown. Drain, crumble and set aside. Place beef, sausage and garlic in skillet and cook over medium-high heat until well done. Drain grease. Mix in onion and cook until tender. Stir in brown sugar, syrup, ketchup, mustard and chipotle sauce. Reduce heat to medium-low. Bring to a boil and cook 20 minutes, stirring often.

Mix bacon, baked beans, kidney beans, black beans, pinto beans, and lentils into skillet. Continue cooking 20 minutes. Preheat oven to 350 degrees F (175 degrees C). Line a baking sheet with aluminum foil. Season beans with chili powder and salt. Pour mixture into a large casserole dish and place on prepared baking sheet on lowest rack of preheated oven. Bake 30 minutes. Let stand 10 minutes before serving.

Montreal Steak-Seasoned Mashed Potatoes

Ingredients

>   3 pounds red potatoes cut into chunks
>   1/4 cup butter
>   3 ounces cream cheese, cut into pieces
>   1/4 cup milk
>   4 tablespoons bacon bits
>   1/2 cup shredded Colby-Monterey Jack cheese
>   2 tablespoons Montreal steak seasoning
>   1/2 teaspoon kosher salt, or to taste

Directions

Place the potatoes into a large pot and cover with salted water. Bring to a boil over high heat, then reduce heat to medium-low, cover, and simmer until tender, about 20 minutes. Drain. Mash the potatoes with a potato masher; mash in butter and cream cheese. Stir in milk, bacon bits, Colby-Jack cheese, and steak seasoning. Season to taste with salt.

Stuffed Filet Mignon Mini-Bites

Ingredients
   4 (6 ounce) filet mignon steaks
   1 (16 ounce) bottle Italian dressing
   1 (8 ounce) package cream cheese
   1/4 cup minced jalapeno pepper
   1 clove garlic, diced finely
   20 slices thinly sliced bacon
Directions

Slice the steaks into 1/2-inch wide strips. Pound the strips to about half their original thickness. Place the steak in a bowl; pour the Italian dressing and garlic over the meat; allow to marinate at least 2 hours. Mix together the cream cheese and jalapeno peppers in a bowl; set aside. Remove the strips from the marinade and lay out on a flat surface. Spread about 1 teaspoon of the cream cheese mixture on each strip.

Preheat an outdoor grill for high heat and lightly oil grate. Remove the strips from the marinade and lay on a flat surface. Spread about 1 teaspoon of the cream cheese mixture on each strip. Fold the meat around the cream cheese mixture to form a ball.

Wrap each ball with a slice of bacon. Secure bacon with water-soaked toothpicks or metal skewers.

Cook on preheated grill until steak is no longer pink, a minimum of 4 minutes per side.

Tangy Bacon-y Sirloin Strips

Ingredients
    1/4 cup vegetable oil
    2 tablespoons Worcestershire sauce
    1 garlic clove, minced
    1/2 teaspoon onion powder
    1/2 teaspoon salt
    1/4 teaspoon pepper
    1 pound (1 inch thick) boneless sirloin steak
    8 bacon strips
    Lemon-pepper seasoning
    GLAZE:
    1/2 cup barbecue sauce
    1/2 cup steak sauce
    1/3 cup stir fry sauce
    1/3 cup hoisin sauce
    1/2 cup honey
    1 tablespoon molasses
    Directions
    In a large re-sealable plastic bag, combine the first six ingredients. Cut steak into four wide strips; add to the marinade. Seal bag and turn to coat; refrigerate for 2-3 hours or overnight, turning once. Drain and discard marinade. Wrap a bacon strip around each steak piece; secure with a toothpick. Sprinkle with lemon-pepper. Coat grill rack with non-stick cooking spray before starting the grill. Grill steak, covered, over medium-low heat for 10-15 minutes, turning occasionally, until meat reaches desired doneness (for medium-rare, a meat thermometer should read 145 degrees F; medium, 160 degrees F; well-done, 170 degrees F).

Combine the glaze ingredients; brush over steaks. Grill until glaze is heated. Discard toothpicks.

Seriously Stuffed Mushrooms

Ingredients
   1 (8 ounce) package cream cheese, softened
   2/3 cup barbeque sauce
   3 tablespoons steak sauce
   3 drops Angostura bitters
   1 (8 ounce) package fresh mushrooms, stems removed
   1 cup bacon bits
Directions
   Preheat oven to 400 degrees F (200 degrees C). Lightly grease a 9x13 inch baking dish. In a medium bowl, mix together cream cheese, half of the bacon bits bitters, barbeque sauce and steak sauce.

   Arrange mushroom caps in the baking dish, and stuff each cap with equal portions of the cream cheese mixture. Sprinkle with rest of bacon bits.

   Bake 10 to 15 minutes in the preheated oven, or until lightly browned.

Colorado Styled Lobster

Ingredients
4 (8 ounce) beef tenderloin filets
salt and pepper to taste
1/2 teaspoon garlic powder
4 slices bacon
1/2 cup butter, divided
1 teaspoon OLD BAY® Seasoning
8 ounces lobster tail, cleaned and chopped
Directions
Set oven to Broil at 500 degrees F (260 degrees C).

Sprinkle tenderloins all over with salt, pepper, and garlic powder. Wrap each filet with bacon, and secure with a toothpick. Place on a broiling pan, and broil to desired doneness, about 8 to 10 minutes per side for medium rare.

While tenderloins are cooking, melt 1/4 cup of butter over medium heat with 1/2 teaspoon Old Bay® seasoning. Stir in chopped lobster meat, and cook until done. Spoon lobster meat over cooked tenderloins, and return them to the broiler until the lobster meat begins to brown.

While the lobster is in the oven, heat the remaining 1/4 cup of butter in a small saucepan over medium-high heat, cook until it browns, turning the color of a hazelnut. To serve, spoon the browned butter over the steaks, and sprinkle with the remaining Old Bay® seasoning.

The Bacon Award Winning Chili

Ingredients
- 1 (14.5 ounce) can stewed tomatoes, chopped
- 1 (6 ounce) can tomato paste
- 1 carrot, sliced
- 1 onion, chopped
- 2 stalks celery, chopped
- 1/4 cup white wine
- 1 pinch crushed red pepper flakes
- 1/4 cup chopped green bell pepper
- 1/4 cup chopped red bell pepper
- 1/3 cup bottled steak sauce
- 12 slices bacon
- 1 1/2 pounds ground beef
- 1 (1.25 ounce) package chili seasoning mix
- 1 teaspoon ground cumin
- 1 (15 ounce) can kidney beans, drained
- 1 tablespoon chopped fresh cilantro
- 1 tablespoon chopped fresh parsley

Directions

In a large pot over medium-low heat, combine tomatoes, tomato paste, carrot, onion, celery, wine, pepper flakes, bell peppers and steak sauce.

While tomato mixture is simmering, cook bacon in a large skillet over medium heat until crisp. Remove to paper towels. Cook beef in bacon drippings until brown; drain. Stir chili seasoning into ground beef.

Stir seasoned beef, cumin and bacon into tomato mixture. Continue to simmer until vegetables are tender and flavors are well blended. Stir in beans, cilantro and parsley. Heat through and serve.

Whiskey Steak

2 pounds beef round steak, 1 inch thick
   salt and pepper to taste
   2 cloves garlic, crushed
   1/3 cup sweet-hot mustard, divided
   8 slices bacon
   1 tablespoon olive oil, or as needed
   3 tablespoons chopped fresh rosemary
   2/3 cup bourbon whiskey
   2 tablespoons Worcestershire sauce
   1 tablespoon brown sugar
   1 tablespoon lemon juice
   Directions

Season the steaks on both sides with salt and pepper. In a small bowl, mix together the garlic and all but 2 teaspoons of the mustard. Place the steaks on a plate, and spread half of the garlic mustard mixture over one side of them. Let stand for 30 minutes. Heat a large skillet over medium-high heat. Fry bacon until crisp, then remove from the pan, leaving the grease. Crumble the bacon and set aside.

Heat the bacon grease in the skillet over medium-high heat, and add olive oil if necessary to cover the bottom of the pan. Fry steaks mustard side down for about 5 minutes, until golden brown. While the steaks are frying, spread the remaining garlic and mustard over the top. Flip the steaks over, and fry for about 2 minutes, until browned. Remove steaks to a serving platter, and keep warm.

Keep the skillet over medium-high heat, and stir in the rosemary, whiskey, reserved mustard, Worcestershire sauce, brown sugar, and lemon juice. Simmer for about 2 minutes. Top steaks with crumbled bacon and the sauce, and serve.

Manly Steak

Ingredients

2 (8 ounce) beef rib-eye steaks, cut 3/4 inch thick
1 teaspoon steak seasoning
6 thick slices bacon
2 teaspoons butter
1/4 teaspoon Worcestershire sauce
5 drops Angostura bitters
3/4 teaspoon Dijon mustard
1/2 cup thinly sliced red bell pepper
8 ounces small mushrooms, quartered
2 tablespoons crumbled blue cheese
2 cloves garlic, diced finely

Directions

Prepare an outdoor grill using charcoal briquettes stacked 2 to 3 deep. Season the steaks on both sides with steak seasoning.

While the charcoal heats up, fry the bacon in a skillet over medium-high heat until crisp. Remove from the skillet and drain on paper towels. Leave grease in the pan.

When the charcoal is covered with gray ashes, put the steaks on the grill. Cook for 12 minutes, turning once, or to your desired degree of doneness.

While the steaks are cooking, stir the butter, bitters, Worcestershire sauce and mustard into the bacon grease. Cook and stir over medium-high heat until butter has melted. Add the red bell pepper, garlic and mushrooms; cook and stir until tender.

To serve, place steaks onto plates. Top with bacon, then blue cheese and then the vegetables. Serve immediately.

Dudes! Let's start a Manly Bromance!

Dudes don't let other dudes go without the Manly Cookbooks. Liked what you found in this cookbook? You can let other dudes know! Give us 5 stars and leave a rave review!

- This is book one of the Manly Cookbook Series. Look for the other books in the series, such as Beef and Bar-B-Q, Chicken and Poultry, and more to come.
- Want to get in touch? Email us at ManlyCookbooks@gmail.com
- You can get the deets on more books from the Manly Cookbook Series if you like and share our Facebook Page: https://www.facebook.com/ManlyCookbooks
- Follow and retweet us on Twitter to get a heads-up on when our books are free on Amazon Kindle! https://twitter.com/ManlyCookbooks
- And your best way to stay in touch is to Sign up on using the form below to receive alerts when our eBooks are free or for special deals. https://docs.google.com/forms/d/1qlMGtMAXXeFkQV R0h5_zFZYVdR6GAoHNiBRdt_wznbg/viewform?usp= send_form
- We respect your privacy. You will never receive spam from us. Manly recipes? Yes. Spam? Heck no.

Thanks for reading! Now get to Manly cooking.
Sincerely

Chew Man-Food
Chew Man-Food

Author of all books in the Manly Cookbook Series.

PS. This book was generously promoted by The Bacon Chronicle. The Bacon Chronicle is devoted to bringing you the best sizzling recipes, the latest bacon news, the meatiest festival coverage, and much more. Go pig or go home!

Connect with them at the sites below to find out more about their fun Bacon promotions:

Website: www.baconchronicle.com

Twitter: www.twitter.com/BaconChronicle

Facebook: www.facebook.com/BaconChronicle

Did you love *The Manly Cookbook: Bacon*? Then you should read *The Manly Cookbook: Beef and Bar-B-Q* by Chew Man-Food!

Steaks, roasts, stir fry. Top it off with anything you can throw on the barbecue and you get this next installment of the Manly Cookbook series. Find 75+ tried and true recipes with beef or made on the bar-b-q. Men (and women with a taste for everything manly), don't even try to stop drooling. It is inevitable.
Let's get to it!

Also by Chew Man-Food

The Manly Cookbook Series
The Manly Cookbook: Bacon
The Manly Cookbook: Beef and Bar-B-Q

CPSIA information can be obtained
at www.ICGtesting.com
Printed in the USA
FFOW04n1019311215
20073FF